Living with Waves

poems by

Megan Griffin

Finishing Line Press
Georgetown, Kentucky

Living with Waves

*I dedicate this collection to Jared, Glenice, and Eileen.
I am grateful to have known you and
share just a fraction of your stories.*

Copyright © 2025 by Megan Griffin
ISBN 979-8-89990-006-8 First Edition
All rights reserved under International and Pan-American Copyright Conventions. No part of this book may be reproduced in any manner whatsoever without written permission from the publisher, except in the case of brief quotations embodied in critical articles and reviews.

ACKNOWLEDGMENTS

Thank you to the editors of Months to Years magazine for publishing "Survivor of Suicide Loss Quiz."

Publisher: Leah Huete de Maines
Editor: Christen Kincaid
Cover Art: Megan Griffin
Author Photo: Allegra Anderson Photography
Cover Design: Elizabeth Maines McCleavy

Order online: www.finishinglinepress.com
also available on amazon.com

Author inquiries and mail orders:
Finishing Line Press
PO Box 1626
Georgetown, Kentucky 40324
USA

Contents

I. The Flood

Committed 1

If I'm Being Honest 2

Questions for Us 3

II. The Whirlpool

An Empty Chair at the Table 7

When I Go 9

The Glue 11

III. The Mist

Wishes for Us 15

The Pictures Remain 17

Lady at the Lake 20

IV. Swimming through Tides

Survivor of Suicide Loss Quiz 25

Best to Stay Busy 27

Resilient 29

Birth After Death 31

The Flood

Committed

    Cold sheets on your empty bed.
    Ominous walls that heard too
   much. Saw you sleeping, your
   mind both overloaded and vacant.
  I wonder how that works
 toying with opposites and denying
tears, like a dam
ensuring pressure builds but
does not release.

Could it be that it was an accident
 or just a moment where it became too much?
  Maybe there was something we could have done
   Medication just wasn't enough.
    I didn't know how to help you and
     tell you my support was unconditional.
      To think that others view you as selfish
       enrages me. You didn't commit a sinful crime. You
        dared to end your pain, which I eventually forgave.

If I'm Being Honest

Our mother cycles pictures
whenever she feels or
when another year has gone.

She shares moments
of gold when his smile
was wide and real.
Creates an illusion
the screams and cuts
have washed away.

Every swipe of her feed
conjures his name
to the forefront
of my mind
in moments I
desire an identity
of my own.

Longing to get back missed chances
of letting loose, dancing free,
and romance
I denied myself
after his death.

In these moments
I wear a mask
of gratitude
to hide
a harsh truth.

If I'm being honest
now I know
it is possible
to be jealous
of the dead.

Questions for Us

Are you in the basement?
Where the dark cobwebbed corners
made it a dungeon
but the bright lights in the center
made it a playground.
Where we rode bikes around
Daddy's work table
and grabbed our sleds at the
first signs of New England snow.

I don't go down there anymore.

Are you in your room?
Where your laugh once bounced
against the walls covered
in cartoon posters, the yellow
of the Minions brighter against
the blue of your wall.
Where we searched for signs
of you as we cleared it.
Sock by sock, sweatshirt by sweatshirt.

I don't visit there anymore.

How long were you planning it for?
I fear it may have been
as long, or longer, than I wondered
if that was your fate. Every nap
that lasted too long
or the absence of sound
behind your closed door.

Are you mad how we buried you?
Amid the small markers of ill infants
in an 18th century cemetery
your evergreen headstone

sticking out like a spiky starfish
amidst dull mussels.

Where can I go to find you?

People ask
Do you have any siblings?

I don't like my answer anymore.

I tell them yes, but that
you're gone.

II. The Whirlpool

An Empty Chair at the Table

As she drifted away
peacefully that November,
she won.
Pain and morphine battled
each other inside of her
but they both lost.

Days after the leader she despised
was voted out
and just two weeks shy
of what should have been
her last Thanksgiving.

We trusted
it would happen
after the lilacs bloomed.
More than half a year left
and another birthday
waiting to be celebrated.

Soon her determination to
be at my graduation
seemed far from reach.
But eating Dominos together
that Christmas Eve seemed
so real we could feel the taste.

We knew by the election
her doctor's *Probably in the spring*
was out the window.
Fluffy eggs. The last thing she ate.
Drips of morphine. The last thing she tasted.

Thanksgiving came.
Our stomachs were full
but we were empty.

Like her seat
at the table and car
in the driveway
idle and vacant.

When I Go

You only talked about things.
Pillows,
pictures,
a ceramic polar bear.

Writing names on the bottom
and pointing with your
arthritis ridden finger
showing each person
what was rightfully theirs
in your eyes.

Don't forget, when I go this goes to you!

We never talked about the hole.
One that the stuff can't fill.

The empty chair at the table.
Silence in place of your laugh.
No Happy Birthday to sing
the second week of January.

The phone without a ring
just to check in.
A clear schedule, rid of the drive
to and from check-ups and shots.
The pill case on your nightstand
sitting empty.

There's a picture of us
from 2001
on my desk. You're
wearing a shirt
with three animal
prints while your
eyes smile at me.

I wonder where
that shirt is now.
More than a piece
of fabric, a piece
of you.

The Glue

The excitement
was tangible
in the high-pitched comfort of
of her jubilant giggles.

Always seeking a
break in the dark clouds.
Mostly for others,
rarely herself.

Master of any job
strict bus driver turned
dutiful nanny and
active store manager.

Mother and grandmother.
The most difficult jobs
of all. Decades
which could never
be repaid.

On calls for
hours yearning
to fizzle out
sparks
of the lifelong fires
in a family
who fights with passion.

Her last Mother's Day
wearing a mask
white as the grin
it covered. Grey
and thinning hair
souvenirs from
the unwanted constants
chemo and COVID.

Two dominating forces
opposing the core
of her being.

A comforting constant.
Stubborn and sweet.

The Mist

Wishes for Us

I wish I could tell you
how I'm feeling
what I've accomplished
where I've been.

I wish I could tell you
about my moments of despair
when I longed for
your familiar comfort
and began to accept a world
without the you I knew.

I wish you could tell me
the words that are trapped
in your failing brain.
Blunt ones that could
get you in trouble or
comforting ones that could
calm me.
With the same lips
that still stretch wide
when you laugh.

I wish you could tell me
stories of your youth
calming wisdom
that is stuck
inside of you.

I wish I could tell you
how proud I am
to have known you.
That I am who I am
because of you.

I wish I could tell you
I live by the motto
Support Your Local Feminist,
which is imprinted on my mind
just as it was on the sign
at the top of your basement door.

The Pictures Remain

Red Oak Hill Studio is the name of Eileen's independent photography company, an extension to her identity besides Nana, Mom, and therapist. Each red leaf stamp on the back of her photographs was a seal of approval. Signifying Eileen's acceptance of her eye for nature. She didn't have an actual studio, but she did live on Red Oak Hill Road. Where her sunroom had photos sprawled across all the furniture. Ready for matting and framing before they were sold at an annual local artist's event. For the 2x3 photos, Eileen gathered textured card paper and glued her photos in the center. As dementia set in and her memory faded, many cards were left unfinished without her classic signature on the front and stamp on the back.

I. The Reading Fairy

Eileen's eye latches on to it as more than a statue, as she sees some of herself in this small mythical girl made of stone. The "reading fairy" sits on top of a column and is content with the book sprawled across her lap. A monarch butterfly sits right on top of the fairy's leaf hat. Wings spread wide open. Both the fairy and monarch stand out with personality among the large green leaves that surround them. Kind of like how Eileen does with her unique fashion and blunt remarks. Eileen is proud of capturing this moment. She prints it in endless sizes to sell and gift it to those who share her joy of reading and admire the possibility of fairies. What the photo doesn't show is the butterfly using its weightless wings to take flight moments later. But the fairy statue remains in place with wings of stone carved into her back. Eileen comes to know this feeling years later when her hands, legs, and mind slow down. Eventually becoming familiar with the struggle of being stuck.

II. The Stone Church Windows

In Colorado, Eileen visits nature that resembles a different universe from the one she grew up in. But on this visit, it is the interior landscapes that catch her eye. She comes across two windows in a stone church. They are surrounded by darkness as light beams through them. Each window is an arch, a shape which presents itself as an entrance to something. The rippled texture and vibrant colors make each pane opaque. The exterior landscape is not visible, and the only thing Eileen knows is behind them is the light of day. The window is not an entrance, but instead a barrier between the outside world and the church's sacred bubble. Eileen's eyes were a clear window once, revealing her thoughts with a glimmer, squint, or eye roll. Over time they became more like the stone church windows, still radiating their blue beauty but unable to reveal anything behind them.

III.   Adirondack Monarchs

Every summer, Eileen manages to capture new crevices of the Adirondacks. Sometimes all it takes is a drive down the road with stops along the way to observe what creatures or insects were latched on to the local wildflowers. At the height of the monarch migration, she finds clusters of asters serving as the rest stops for groups of tired wings. With thin pink petals and a prickly yellow center, the asters are much smaller than the reading fairy's hat yet they provide the monarchs with nutrients. Eileen captures action photos of them claiming their nectar with wings three times the size of one flower. One monarch spreads its deep orange wings on display for Eileen's camera. In this light they are translucent, showing a blurry silhouette of the aster they are gripping on to. Over the years, Eileen's brain becomes blurry too as she is covered by the mask of dementia. She may no longer look and act as she did when she captured this moment with the monarchs, but fleeting moments reveal that parts of the once blooming Eileen is still there inside.

IV.   Calm Branches

In Eileen's backyard, all the trees lost their leaves a month ago. She captures one tree with the clear powder blue sky as a backdrop, a welcome surprise the day after a rainstorm. Eileen captures this simplicity for herself and those who made decades of memories with her under these branches. There are more branches than she had imagined when the leaves were covering them. They are naked and free. Ready to catch the imminent snow. The sun is her assistant as it illuminates the water droplets clinging on the branches after the early winter rainstorm. With no clouds in sight, they shine like twinkly white Christmas lights. As the day goes on, the droplets fall as the branches shake just like Eileen's hands. As her motor skills slow, she develops tremors and can only hold a small simple camera to capture this fleeting moment.

V. Autumn Waterfall

Eileen puts her camera away when her mind begins to slip. She moves away from Red Oak Hill and to The Ivy for better care. Her husband Gary visits to remind her of who she is and what she used to do. He brings family photos which distract her from the white mask that hides his smile and muffles his laugh. Eileen's mind is working slower now, so she struggles to respond to Gary's jokes that accompany his presentation of each photo. He shows her one last photo, this time replacing a joke with a serious question: "Do you know who took this?" Gary looks at her afraid that she won't be able to respond, yet with hope that the answer is in her. The photo shows a large waterfall cascading between green, orange, and yellow leaves. Clearly somewhere remote. A beauty only attained through the effort of hiking. With a surprising speed, Eileen knows the answer. She points to herself with a smirk and says "Me!" Gary is thrilled that she remembers, but it was a different reaction than he would have expected from the Eileen he knew for decades. When she had more words, she would have said "Oh Gary. Come on! I took that years ago in the Adirondacks. Don't you remember?"

Lady at the Lake

I know the Nana
breathing in August air
flowing across the lake
as the sun rays peek
around the trees
illuminating her on
the screened-in porch.

She looks at hummingbirds
fluttering for their nectar
then places a bookmark
between the pages
she just savored.

I know the Nana
who walks carefully
down a steep hill
to her boathouse
then breathes relief
on her dock
as she hears
the peace of
summer clearly.

While she swims
a soft wail
from the bay
urges her to break
her own silence
Oh there's a loon!
A tranquil bird
that pulls her back
to the water
every summer.

I don't know the girl
that moved around
New England
nine times, with strict
parents and tough
siblings. Seven years old
standing in front
of Niagara Falls
used to the labor
of starting over.

I don't know the young woman
who posed in white
with elegant gloves
and flowers. Pretty
for the professor who courted
her as a secretary. They twirl
to *The Tennessee Waltz*
as she's unaware
of the obstacles she'll face
in a marriage that lasts
over half a century.

I don't know the mother
pushing for her education,
studying while her kids
run in the yard. Taking
tests more than once.
Gleaming pride
through her smile
each time she graduates.

I don't know the feminist
social worker dedicated
to community projects

and clients she saw
in her serene sunroom.

I don't know the empty-nester
thirsty for travel
dragging her husband
from France to New Zealand.
Her film capturing
each moment made
in front of the mountains.

I wish I had known
the moving girl
naïve bride
learning mother
and feminist social worker.

Sometimes I forget
she is more
than the lady at the lake.

Swimming through Tides

Survivor of Suicide Loss Quiz

1. When a person loses a loved one to suicide, who will be there for them?
    1. Family experiencing the same loss
    2. Childhood friends
    3. Past teachers
    4. The ones they least expected

2. Define "the easy way out."

3. Which term best describes the feeling when a person realizes they will never see their loved one again?
    1. Persistent denial
    2. Sucker punch
    3. Confusing anger
    4. Limbless

4. Define "resilient"

5. How many casseroles will be dropped off at their house by people with knowing looks of sorrow?
    1. Too many
    2. 1 for every person that has no idea how to help
    3. A dozen in the first week
    4. None in the fifth week

6. What is the best statement religious acquaintances deliver as words of comfort?
    1. "May God be with you in these troubling times."
    2. "Always remember, God grant me the serenity..."
    3. "God has a plan for your life. This is just a bump in the road."
    4. "They're in a better place, home with God. Nothing can hurt them now."

7. What does the person do when people make jokes about suicide?
    1. Wince inside, stay silent
    2. Politely walk away

3. Keep scrolling, there's no mental energy left to combat that today
4. Screams, cries, and educates

8. Define "trauma"

9. Define "survivor"

10. What does the person say when people ask "Oh no. How did they pass?"
    1. "They killed themselves."
    2. Smiles uncomfortably, "I'd rather not say."
    3. "They died by suicide."
    4. "The epidemic of depression, anxiety, and despair."

11. How does the person celebrate holidays?
    1. Begrudgingly
    2. Joyfully
    3. Reluctantly
    4. Puts on a fake smile, as they glance at the empty chair next to them, then passes the turkey

12. How does the person remember their loved one on the anniversary of their death?
    1. Cries on the couch, scrolling on social media flooded with joyful yet painful pictures
    2. Orders a cheeseburger sub and takes a walk by the beach
    3. Visits the snow-covered cemetery, holds in the tears until they walk away from the shining dark-green headstone
    4. All of the above

13. When do they stop thinking about their loved one?
    1. In fleeting moments of joy
    2. While engrossed in an intense movie
    3. On a road trip to Canada
    4. Never

Best to Stay Busy

Week fifty-eight
and you're still
treading water. Tempted
to stop and drown
in mourning.

Grief doesn't care
how long you've
been lost who
you are or
what you do.

Week two
comforting casseroles
from people who say

It's best to go back
to work, school,
and life.

It's what they
would want
you to do.

Week one
completing rituals.
Pick an urn. Plan
the funeral. Smile
for distant family
who pay
their respects
but don't know
what to say.

The 19th Century
said widows should
mourn longer than others.
At least a year
suffices to be veiled
in a black dress
and clouded mind.

Wipe your tears.
Go to sleep.
Eat three meals.
The one-size-fits-all
prescription.

Don't stop.
Don't break.
Don't think.
Just do.

Resilient

Some people are more resilient.
They don't require breaks,
like a cool fridge
always running. Fulfilling
its purpose and tasks
around the clock.

Until one day it starts
to heat up and sweat
dripping on old
jars of salsa
shoved and buried
in the back of the shelf.

I wonder
if the condensation
is salty?
Like the hot tears
I lick
off my less
resilient mouth.

Some people compare their strength
on a scoreboard of mourning.

How many tears
panic attacks
sleepless nights
and flashbacks
did you have this week?

How many days
did you call out of work
after your fleeting days
of bereavement
were up?

When did you
stop forgetting
they are dead?
Thinking
they were about to
roll out of bed
walk through the door
or ask for a hug.

Tally your score.
It should be enough
to show
you care
but not too much
to show
you're consumed.

Effects of grief change
like the weather.
Through fast downpours
slow heatwaves
and whirlwind hurricanes.

All grieving people are resilient.

Birth After Death

Our lives start
surrounded by fluid.
We can't walk
talk or swim yet
we know the comfort
of being wrapped
up by wavy molecules.

We enter the world
after the water breaks.

Some of us
are rushed in to
the unfamiliar
harsh cold air.

Some of us
find solace
as we slide in to
a pool of water.

At the start of
my grief
I'm obsessed with
the birth process. One
of the few experiences
we all endure
yet can't remember.

I wonder if
the method of our birth
has an impact on us
beyond medical knowledge.

My best friend says
You should be a doula!
She hears the passion

in my voice
every time I talk
about birth.

As my grief
evolves my odd
fascination fades.

Through death I was reborn.
I had to birth
myself. Break
my own water
and dive into
the pool of life.

Megan Griffin is an emerging writer from the Quiet Corner of Connecticut whose work explores the themes of grief and nature. She earned a BA in professional writing from Bay Path University and MA in English from Bridgewater State University. Megan's work has been published in *Barrelhouse, Brevity, Months to Years,* and *Sad Girl Diaries. Living with Waves* is her first poetry collection.

www.ingramcontent.com/pod-product-compliance
Lightning Source LLC
Chambersburg PA
CBHW030051100426
42734CB00038B/1220